CW00448702

IMAGES OF ENGLAND

Around Malton

Malton Wesleyan Church Choir, 16th April 1916. Back row, left to right: Firth Jenson, Annie North, W.P. Snow, Bernard Snow, -?-, George Johnson, -?-. Middle row, left to right: -?-, E. Snowball, -?-, Rose Cattle, Mr Hollings, Clarice Cattle, T.N. Hargreaves. Front row, left to right: Lily Sadler, Nora Hollings, George Gibson.

IMAGES OF ENGLAND

Around Malton

John Stone

NONSUCH

Voting in the Buckrose District of the East Riding, *c.* 1906.

First published 1996
This new pocket edition 2005
Images unchanged from first edition

Nonsuch Publishing Limited
The Mill, Brimscombe Port,
Stroud, Gloucestershire, GL5 2QG
www.nonsuch-publishing.com

© John Stone, 1996

The right of John Stone to be identified as the Author
of this work has been asserted in accordance with the
Copyrights, Designs and Patents Act 1988.

British Library Cataloguing in Publication Data.
A catalogue record for this book is available from the British Library.

ISBN 1-84588-118-4

Typesetting and origination by Nonsuch Publishing Limited
Printed in Great Britain by Oaklands Book Services Limited

Contents

The building of Wentworth Street.

Acknowledgements

My thanks to those who kindly loaned me photographs and postcards and gave me information about some of the town's history: Mr William Searle, Mr Patrick Noble, Mr Paul Taylor, Mr Noel Goodwill and also the local libraries.
I would also like to thank my family for their help and support.
The remainder of the information, pictures and postcards are taken from my own collection.

Introduction

Malton has a long history, going back to the Parisi Settlement in the Stone Age period. It was called Derventio by the Romans, who arrived in AD 71 and departed AD 429. The Saxons called it Meldun, pronounced Maiden and one of the boundaries is still called Maiden Greve Balk. In the Domesday Book we are Maltune. Later when Eustace Fitz-John built a new town around his castle, we became New Malton. Old Malton village is the site of the original town.

When the Romans were here we were the oldest town-fort north of the Humber, they left a large fort in the Orchard Fields but this was demolished in the early 1800s to make way for a Fair or Gala field. The Castle stood where the Lodge Gardens are today; it was originally of wood which Archbishop Thurstan's Army besieged and burnt to the ground, in 1135, because Eustace Fitz-John delivered his castles of Alnwick and Malton to David King of Scotland. Later he was reconciled with King Stephen and rebuilt the Castle and Town Walls in stone. By this time he did not require the Manor of Old Malton, so he handed it over to Canons of the Ghilbertine Order. After the dissolution Robert Holgate, Archbishop of York in 1546 founded a Grammar School at the Old Malton Priory. During the reign of Henry II (1154–89) Roger-de-Flamvill founded a Hospital of St Nicholas at the foot of the bridge and placed it under control of the Canons of Malton.

In 1322, Robert the Bruce occupied the castle, after which it slowly fell into ruins. Later it came in to the possession of the Eure family and Lord Eure built a house in 1569, and a replacement was built in 1604. In 1674 it became the property of two sisters who disagreed over ownership, so the mansion was pulled down by order of the Court and the materials divided between them. The Estate was sold to Sir Thomas Wentworth in 1712. The estate passed to Earl Fitzwilliam in 1782 and is still in the possession of the Fitzwilliams today.

King Charles and Queen Henrietta stayed here in 1643. A Hunting Lodge was required by the Strickland family in 1684 and is now part of the Talbot Hotel. Malton was a very industrial town. The river Derwent was used by vessels in the 1700s. Gas lights were in shops and streets by 1834. In 1845 the railway arrived and Malton grew. We had Rose's, Russell and Wrangham and Crystal Brewerys. At one time Malton, Norton and Old Malton had 66 hotels, public and beer houses. Russell's Flour Mills, together with other mills and the livestock market, flourished.

Norton and its vicinity are noted for their extensive and well-appointed training and breeding establishments for racehorses and is one of the largest training centres in the North of England. Besides the training ground, there was a regular steeplechase course which had been in use from the 1700s. Racing and racehorses are still the life blood of the district.

The following pictures give us an insight into their lives and times.

Aerial view, showing the river and railway.

One

About Town

Yorkersgate. The Gate Inn is on the right-hand side, with Blair's shop at the corner of Saville Street.

Yorkersgate and The George Hotel with its archway. Opposite, the archway to Dodsworth's work shops. Timber came by boat, and was carried up Water Lane and across to the workshops. The building (left), with railings, is the Corn Exchange.

Yorkersgate. On the right is the Post Office. It moved from Chancery Lane, to Post Office Corner (Butcher Corner) in 1888, and later moved to Wheelgate in 1911. The impressive building on the left is the Savings Bank.

The War Memorial and Cannon. The Cannon was placed here in 1883, and was captured in 1855 at Sebastopol during the Crimean War.

The Talbot Hotel, converted from a Hunting Lodge (c. 1684) and owned by the Strickland family.

York Road, looking from Malton. This was part of the Turnpike road from York.

Castle Howard Road. On the right hand side behind the hedge was Longster's Orchard.

Middlecave Road. This road leads to the hospital and the Grammar School.

Market Place. The coach outside the Town Hall is the Leavening Bus Service. The van is advertising, Calvert's Pure Yorkshire Beef Dripping.

High side of the Market Place. The man with the 'X' is Mr Marshall leaving the bank. Note the carrier's carts awaiting passengers and goods to be taken back to the surrounding villages.

This is Fitch & Co., millinery showrooms at the bottom of the Market Place, now Paley's shop. The Royal Oak Public House and the Balloon Yeast Stores can also be seen.

Market Place, looking up to the Town Hall. The cart is advertising, Gold Medal Balloon Yeast. In the centre of the picture on the right of the Town Hall, the Bull Hotel can be seen.

The Town Hall, which now houses the Malton Museum. This is a sixteenth-century building with a market hall. The Justice's Room above was enlarged in 1856, and a fire nearly destroyed it in 1877. Note the Bull Hotel which has now been demolished.

Street Scene, MALTON. YORKS.

Finkle Street from the Market Place. The Bull Hotel on the right, now demolished for Newgate, stood next to the Criterion Public House.

Finkle Street. All the right hand side was demolished in 1935. Boyes Store stands on the site of Bower's Cafe, which stood on the site of the Prince of Wales Hotel.

Newbiggin – so named because it was a 'new beginning', outside the City Walls. Looking up Newbiggin, the white building on the right is the Blue Ball Inn.

Wheelgate with Bower's butchers shop on the left. Next door is the Meadow Dairy, which is on the site of the Castle Howard Ox, closed in the 1920s. On the right is the Cross Keys and the building with the two spires was the Methodist Chapel until 1951.

Wheelgate with The Clarence public house. The shop is Wardill's Saddlers, still a saddler's shop today.

Wheelgate viewed before the introduction of the motor car, c. 1905.

Wheelgate, viewed in the 1930s when the motor car was firmly established.

Butcher Corner, showing Snow's shop. The Snow family owned this shop from 1826 until it was demolished for road widening in 1967.

Saville Street. The Temperance & Commercial Hotel is now demolished and Anderson's sport shop stands on the site. Sedman's Outfitters which closed in March 1995, can be seen and above is the Methodist Chapel.

Looking up Old Maltongate to the Estate Office and showing part of the Lodge walls.

One of the gateways to the Lodge.

The Lodge. This is part of a large house and also the site of the Castle. The first house was built by Lord Eure in 1569 and a second house built by Lord Ralph in 1604. It was later inherited by two sisters who could not agreed about ownership in 1674, so the court divided it stone by stone between them. This is all that remains of the Lodge gatehouse.

Mr Barnes Monumental Works at Hope Cottage, Cemetery Road, later to be called Princess Road.

Greengate. St Leonard's Close stands on the site of the now demolished houses on the left. The house behind the lady is the Elephant & Castle.

Looking up Greengate, the large building on the left is Greengate House now owned by Camphill Village Trust.

Wentworth Street, originally called Back Lane. After investigations it has been possible to establish that Wentworth Street was built between 1880 and 1890 but a more precise date has proved elusive.

Castlegate. The four-storey building was demolished c. 1946–9. The next shop is Thomas Taylor's, one of Malton's oldest Tea & Grocery Merchant's, next to Robson's Garage.

Lower Castlegate, originally called Low Street. The shop next door to the white cottage was Mr Fish, saddler.

Castlegate, the white cottages on the previous picture have now been altered into Mr J.T. Foster's shop and cafe. Next to it is the opening called Hawkswell Lane, here was Parker's Garage, later to become Sid Nicholson's.

The river and warehouses from the bridge. All of the centre of the picture is now Railway Street car park.

In 1870, this iron bridge replaced the wooden one built in 1845. A branch line carried goods to the Malton Biscuit Co. mill.

Looking across the river to the tannery on the right hand side.

County Bridge. On the left is the gas works and chimney. The bee hives and garden belong to Mr Goodwill, of the Toll House on the island. One half of it was in the East Riding of Yorkshire, and one half in the North Riding of Yorkshire. This view is taken from the East Riding side.

Malton from the railway bridge. In the centre of the picture is Headley Wise & Son's warehouse, now demolished and replaced with Chandler's Wharf. The building with the lettering is Malton Fire Station.

The railway crossing (York to Scarborough line). In the centre of the picture can be seen Russell's Flour Mill. Note the extra large crossing gate.

Church Street, with Mr J. Jackson & Son, boot and shoe maker and Hornsey & Wood tailors and outfitters.

The Railway Hotel, formally the Bay Horse until 1850. In 1899, Henry Searle demolished the old shops and built the Buckrose Hotel on the site.

Commercial Street, this is the main shopping street of Norton. Norton has grown enormously over the last fifty years but Commercial Street was one of the original streets of the village.

Commercial Street, showing Lowes newsagents. In the centre of the picture, Trinity Chapel can be seen.

Looking back up Commercial Street. Notice the garage with petrol pumps, next door to Mr Redpath, decorator.

The chimneys on the left are on Norton Boys' School. In the centre, the Malt Shovel Hotel, advertising John J. Hunt Ltd., Ebor Ales.

The public house was the Blue Bell, but it was changed in 1857 to the Balaclava and closed in 1972.

Wood Street, half way down on the right is Grove Street, leading to Norton's Girls' School. In the centre of the picture is Wellington House.

Little Wood Street, looking down to the original Hyde Park public house.

Langton Road, looking to St Peter's Church. The road on the right is St Nicholas Street.

Langton Road, (originally called Wold Road). The house in the centre of the picture behind the tree was the Rifleman's Arms public house at the top of Sutton Street. Ness House can also be seen.

A view down St Peter's Street, just off Langton Road, c. 1900.

Eastfield, which is part of the Model Farm council estate, was built in the 1940s.

Mill Street was Green Lane until 1857. At the far end was Victoria Windmill, hence the name.

Beverley Road, where Mill Street and Beverley Road meet. This is the main road to and from Driffield.

Welham Road. The field behind the fence was where wild beast shows were held.
Ruston & Priestman's tan yard in Castlegate brought their bark knots here and used them on the
gallops. On the left, behind the hedge, was C.E. Mennell & Son's sawmill, later to be Taylor Bros.

WELHAM RD NORTON

40

Welham Road, showing Weston Lodge at the opening to The Avenue.

Welham Road looking towards St Peter's Church from the bottom of Whitewall, with not a house in sight.

Beck Mills and pond, which later became a trout hatchery, and is now a housing estate, looking towards St Peter Street.

Beck Mills, a water mill owned by Mr Anderson. This site was mentioned in the Domesday Book.

Highfield Road which divides the Highfield and Peasey Hill estates.

Thatched cottages, Old Malton. This is the Post Office, but these charming cottages have now been demolished. A series of half timber, half brick houses are now built on the site.

Old Malton, looking back up to the thatched cottages.

Old Malton, looking at St Mary's Church. The white building in the centre was where Archbishop Holgate founded a Grammar School in 1547.

Abbey House, built on the ruins of the monastery. Charles Smithson lived here after moving from Easthorpe Hall and was a friend of Charles Dickens.

Two

Shops and Businesses

YORKSHIRE NORTH RIDING

The Dales

Hovingham
8 miles

Castle Howard
5 miles

Harrogate
40 miles

Flamingo
Park Zoo
6 miles

Whitby and
the Moors

Filey
23 miles

Bridlington
28 miles

Malton Market Place

York 18 miles — A 64 — Scarborough 22 miles

**Make MALTON your
Holiday Centre**

Malton, holiday centre of North Riding.

The inside of The Dragon Cafe in the Market Place, now Murray's Cafe.

In the Oak Lounge, the Green Man Hotel, Market Place.

J. Wardill, Saddler and Harness Maker in Wheelgate. This shop is still a saddlers.

W. Sleet, a boot and shoe dealer, in Norton.

K. Inman, one of the butchers in The Shambles, in 1906.

R. Yates & Son, Derwent Foundry, Malton.

R. Yates & Son in Railway Street, established 1845.

Spanton chemist and druggist, in Commercial
Street, Norton stood next door to
Wallgate & Sons.

Buckrose Hotel and S. Wallgate & Sons in Commercial Street.

M. Galtry & Son, a ladies fashion shop in Market Street, 1922 to 1930, was a part of Talbot House.

Mennell's Saddlers, in the Market Place. The present Mennell's now sells luggage items, jewellery and other luxury goods.

Jas Smith & Sons, the dry cleaner's in Yorkersgate. The building today is part of Barclays Bank.

Thomas Taylor & Co., importer's of teas, coffees, and colonial produce, was one of the oldest merchants in town.

Inman Bros., Yorkshire ham and bacon curers, in Commercial Street near to where Norton Library stands today.

Malton Meat Co. in Yorkersgate. The man on the right of the picture is Charlie Wray who later moved to a shop in Wheelgate, near the Post Office.

Dent's green grocers on the corner of Commercial Street and Wold Street is now Fletcher's butchers shop.

Three

The Working Town
and its Transport

The Racecourse, Norton. In 1815, horse racing was attended at this place near Howe Hill. The weighing-in room is still standing.

Highfield Training Stables. Horses trained here by George Searle won at York Races between 1786 and 1794. The new racing complex was owned by the Elsey family.

Whitewall Racing Stables, Welham Road.

Mr Boyce's blacksmith shop in Church Street was later taken over by the Nesfield family. The buildings are now demolished and are part of the entrance to Norton car park.

A horse being shod somewhere in Malton, *c.* 1900.

Horse and cart in Malton, *c.* 1900.

Michaelmas Sheep Fair, which has been held for many years on Malton Showfield. This picture was taken in 1910.

Group of Lincoln Long Wool shearing rams sold at the Michaelmas Sheep Fair, in October, 1910. They were sold by Walter Thompson, Foston, for an average price of £5 4s 0d each.

The Cattle Market was moved here by Earl Fitzwilliam from the Market Square in 1826 who also built a slaughter house. The houses in the centre of the picture have been demolished to make way for the sheep market. The white building is the Spotted Cow. In 1893, the Police Station was built next door on the left which has now become a dentist's.

This bullock is part of the Fat Stock Show in 1903 and is standing outside the old slaughter house (now demolished).

Ponies at the back of Fitch & Co. The gentleman selling the ponies is Mr George Stockdale.

Fitch's cart stating 'Support Home Industry'.

Market Place, showing the market stalls outside St Michael's Church. Carriers' carts can also be seen.

The market and St Michael's Church in the Market Place.

Empty stalls outside St Michael's Church, with the Black Swan in the background.

Inside B.A.T.A., this is the Fleece Sorting Department. This building was originally Malton Biscuit Co., and has now been replaced by a housing complex.

Mr Spanton, with horse and trap, outside the Sun Hotel in Wheelgate. Woolworth's now stands on this site.

Left: The switchboard, at Malton Electric Power Station. In 1904 Electric Lighting was being installed by the Northern Counties Electric Supply Co., Ltd.

Below: Rose's Brewery billhead, which stood in Castlegate.

ESTABLISHED 1767.

190

The Old Brewery MALTON.

TO CHARLES ROSE & Co.

PROPRIETORS:— "J. TROOP."
H. SEDDON.

Part of a hospice to Old Malton Church, now used as a cellar at The Cross Key's Hotel in Wheelgate.

Workpeople outside Russell's Brewery.

Entrance to Camerons 'Russell's Brewery' now demolished and at the entrance to Safeway's Supermarket.

Flood at Russell's Brewery.

Inside the brewery, with Mr E. Biggs.

Delivery wagon for Russell's Brewery. Mr Baxter is holding his son Harry, who later became the Town Crier.

The *VELOCITAS*, a boat converted into a coach, ran between Malton and Hull.

Above: Velocitas Coach, a converted lifeboat which ran from The Angel, Malton to Hull via Driffield, Monday to Thursday at 8.00 a.m. in the 1820s.

Right: Union Coach, ran to York in time for the trains, from the New Globe in 1843. After December 1843 it also ran from the Crown and Anchor, following the opening of the railway (York to Scarborough) in 1845 it stopped running. On the 21st July 1845 it started to run from Malton to Hull.

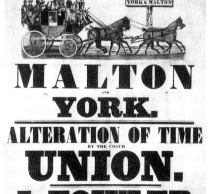

YORK & MALTON

MALTON
AND
YORK.
ALTERATION OF TIME
BY THE COACH
UNION.
J. FOWLER

Begs to inform his Friends and the Public generally, that on and after Monday, December 19th, 1843, he will start from the CROWN & ANCHOR, and the GLOBE Inns, MALTON, every Morning at Eight o'Clock, Sundays excepted, and arrive at York in time for the Trains to LONDON, LEEDS, MANCHESTER, HULL, and SELBY; likewise the Trains for the North : viz., NEWCASTLE, DARLINGTON, NORTH-ALLERTON, and THIRSK.

The Union will return the same Evening at Three o'Clock from Scowen's Railway Hotel, and Dixon's Unicorn Inn, Monk Bar, York, after the arrival of the above Trains.

PARCELS TAKEN ON REASONABLE TERMS.

The Proprietors will not be answerable for any Parcel or Package above the value of Five Pounds, unless entered and paid for accordingly.

Malton Station in the early part of the 1900s.

Malton Station. Note the unique bogey between the lines for passengers to cross to the York platform.

Engine No. 61049 with a train for Whitby arriving at Malton station on 16th August 1963.

Malton's first petrol driven taxi, owned by Alfred Boyes.

Four

Fire, Flood and Pestilence

Malton's first steam fire engine. Monday 21th December 1885 was the christening day of the new fire engine which was made by Messrs Merryweather & Son, London. The steam cylinder of the engine was 5.5 inches in diameter and the pump 4.5inches by 12 inch stroke of steam and the water pistons were capable of pumping 200 gallons per minute. The engine was called The Fitzwilliam.

Above: Saturday, 8th August 1914. Earl Fitzwilliam with Mr and Mrs Hugh Douglas (agent) arrived at the Town Hall and were met by A.L. Russell (Chairman of Malton U.D.C.), W. Kitching (Chairman of Norton U.D.C. and Chairman of the Joint Fire Brigade Committee) and Walter Thompson (Chairman of Malton R.D.C.). Earl Fitzwilliam gave a speech and named the New Fire Engine, Countess Fitzwilliam.

Left: Brown's fire, 2nd March 1910, (The corner of Saville Street and Yorkersgate). The alarm was given, and by 9 o'clock the fire was burning briskly and making its way through the front windows next to Mr Dodsworth's house. The fire descended to Mr Byass's Dairy Shop below and there seemed every prospect of Mr Soulby's Wine & Spirit Stores taking hold. Mr Soulby and Mr Brown were insured but Mr Byass was not.

King's Head fire, 17th April 1913. Malton Market Place was a place of great excitement, a large crowd of people watched one of the worst fires in the town for a long time. The outbreak commenced between 6.30 a.m. and 7 a.m in the rear of the Kings Head kept by Mr Fred Schofield. Flames appeared at the front of the building and swept across the intervening archway carrying the fire to adjoining premises of Mr Foster's Draper's Shop.

Fire Engine, pumping out the Social Services Centre on Norton Road (Black Boards).

Looking up Welham Road with Robson's Garage on the right, Dewhirst Clothing Factory and Ernest Taylor's Sawmills on the left.

Floods in September 1931. On the Saturday night, the water was 14ft above normal and the railway line between Castle Howard and Rillington was closed until the Wednesday. This flood was the highest ever recorded. The previous high flood was in 1878 which showed 1ft more water than in April 1846. Floods outside the Majestic cinema (right) and people in a makeshift boat, outside No. 7 St Nicholas Street (left).

Looking from the bridge to the gasworks (left), and trains standing in flood water (right).

The Railway Station, looking towards Norton railway crossing.

Blackboards or Norton Road, showing Sudderby's bus and Malton's second taxi passing railway waggons.

The floods, taken from the County Bridge, in the 1970s.

A typhoid epidemic broke out in October 1932 and lasted for six weeks. One inmate of the poor house contracted typhoid and it was believed that the disease got into the water supply by a broken drainpipe. During the epidemic, 235 cases were notified and 24 deaths occurred including Dr George Colley Parkin (32) above, who had treated hundreds of people. He left a wife and 2 year old son.

A side view of the Cottage Hospital, which opened in 1905 and contained ten beds and two cots.

The New Hospital, Middlecave, which opened in 1925.

A ward of ten beds in a dining room at Highfield, Norton, during the First World War.

Five

Churches

St Michael's Church, Malton.

St Michael's Church, was built in the twelfth century as a chapel of ease connected to St Mary's at Old Malton.

The Vicarage, in Yorkersgate, belonging to St Michael's Church.

ST. LEONARD CHURCH MALTON.

St Leonard's Church. A twelfth-century chapel of ease connected with St Mary's, Old Malton. Eight Bells were hung on the 5th December 1768. Earl Fitzwilliam gave the clock for Queen Victoria's Diamond Jubilee 1897. It is now being used by the Roman Catholic Church.

The interior of St Leonard's Church, before it became the Roman Catholic church.

St Leonard's vicarage, in Old Maltongate.

The Primitive Methodist Chapel, was built in Wheelgate in 1866 with space for 650 sittings and was demolished in 1951.

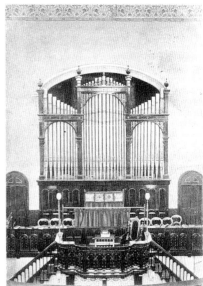

The organ, in the Wesleyan Chapel, Saville Street, which was built in 1811 with 700 sittings.

Catholic Church, Wells Lane, with May Altar, it was built in 1840–1 and dedicated to St Mary.

Bethel Chapel. A piece of land was bought in 'Piccadilly' for £140 12s 6d to build the Bethel Chapel. The stone-laying ceremony took place on Thursday 31st March 1864.

OPENING SERVICES
OF THE
NEW WESLEYAN CHAPEL, NORTON.

On SHROVE TUESDAY, FEB. 16th, 1858,

TWO SERMONS

Will be preached by the Rev. RICHARD ROBERTS, of Leeds,
in the New Chapel, Norton, at Two o'Clock in the Afternoon, and in
the Wesleyan Chapel, Malton, at Half-past Six in the Evening.

ON THE SAME DAY, A
PUBLIC TEA-MEETING

Will be held in the SCHOOL-ROOM, Malton. Tea on the table at
Half-past Four o'Clock. *Tickets, One Shilling each.*

On SUNDAY, FEBRUARY 21st,
SERMONS

Will be preached by the Rev. THOMAS RIGBY, in the Malton
Chapel, at Half-past Ten, and in the Norton Chapel, at Six o'Clock.

And by the Rev. JOHN HICKLING, in the Norton Chapel, at Half-
past Two, and in the Malton Chapel, at Six o'Clock.

On MONDAY, FEBRUARY 22nd,
A LECTURE ON EARLY METHODISM

Will be delivered by the Rev. JOHN HICKLING, in the Malton
Chapel, to commence at Half-past Six o'Clock.

*This aged and venerable Minister is now in his 94th year, is the only one now living
who was sent out by Mr Wesley, and has been seventy years in the ministry.*

**A Collection will be made after each service in aid of the Building Fund
of the Norton Chapel.**

Norton Trinity Methodist Chapel in Commercial Street.

St Nicholas's Church. St Nicholas is the patron Saint of Wayfarers, and many churches were built by fords or bridges. This medieval church, built partly of Roman stone, was demolished in 1814.

St Nicholas Church. This is the second church which was of Grecian style. It had an east window of three lights. The first winter evening service was held on 1st December 1872, when artificial light was installed. The final services were held on 24th June 1891 and it was demolished in 1901.

St Peter's Church, Langton Road. The site of the church was given by Mr R. Wyse, on the 16th October 1889 and the foundation stone was laid and this part of the church completed on 28th June 1894, The rest of the church was not completed until October 1911.

St Peter's vicarage in Langton Road was built in 1904. The vicarage then moved across the road.

OLD MALTON
CHURCH

Old Malton Church of St Mary the Virgin, consists of part of the nave of the
ancient priory founded between 1147 and 1153 by Eustace Fitz-John, for the
Canons of the Gilbertine Order.

Stone coffins, in Old Malton Churchyard. As these coffins were made of stone it suggests they were not used for paupers but for burials of the Gilbertine Order.

The chapels in Old Malton. The Wesleyan was built in 1824 and the Primitive in 1857.

Six

Special Events, Entertainment and Societies

Air Raid Wardens at the bottom end of the Market Place. The policeman is Superintendent Keown.

Malton Boys Brigade attached to Saville Street Chapel in the late 1950s, with Captain Peter Harrison (centre).

Orchard Field Malton 1952.

Raymond Hayes and helpers on the Roman Fort site, in the Orchard Fields 1952.

Empire Day celebrations at Norton Boys School (now the library). Mr Appleton was the head master at the time. This was a day of parades with school children dressed up as children of the Empire countries.

Empire Day and the White Star Band and Boy Scouts outside St Michael's Church in 1914.

Malton Show, is held yearly. It started in 1872, as a flower show at Appleton which became the forerunner of the Appleton and Malton Agriculture Show.

One of the main events of the year was the horse fair, seen here in the early 1900s.

Waiting for the Territorial Army at Malton in 1909.

Lieut.Gen. Baden-Powell opened the new Malton Rifle club in Water Lane 26th March 1908.
At 3 p.m. he arrived at the Town Hall and was met by members of the Urban Council. Then to
Water Lane where boys of the Derwent Cadet Corps lined the route. Lieut.Gen. Baden-Powell
gave a speech, declared the range open and wished the club every success. He also handed over
to the club, a silver Challenge Cup given by Mrs Lupton for competition among the ladies of the
North and East Riding.

The 47th Malton Gala (Thursday 12th July 1906), in Orchard Fields. It rained all morning but by 1 p.m. it was fine for the Military Tournament given by the 18th Hussars and the splendid band of the Regiment. This was their second time in Malton, the year before was a complete washout! In a large tent was a grand show of plants and cut flowers by Messrs Longster & Son and Messrs Slater & Sons.

Malton's first beauty queen, Elsie Owen with Norma Hancox (train bearer) and Valerie Hancox (page) in 1934.

Malton's second beauty queen, Pheobe Buckley with attendants, Ivy Jefferson, Phyllis Linsley, Doris Baines and Gladys Hill in August 1935.

In May 6th 1933, H.R.H Prince George came to open the Social Service Centre, on Norton Road (Blackboards). The building was used later by the Electricity Board.

Fire Brigade parade, 6th May 1905. This was an annual event and in this year it was held at Malton.

Malton White Star Band, at The Club Feast, Fridaythorpe, June 28th, 1907.

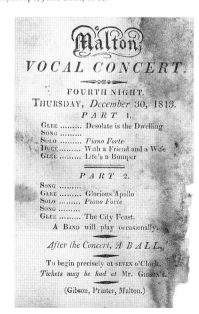

Malton

VOCAL CONCERT.

FOURTH NIGHT.

THURSDAY, *December 30, 1813.*

PART 1.

GLEE .... Desolate is the Dwelling
SONG ....
SOLO .... *Piano Forte*
DUET .... With a Friend and a Wife
GLEE .... Life's a Bumper

PART 2.

SONG ....
GLEE .... Glorious Apollo
SOLO .... *Piano Forte*
SONG ....
GLEE .... The City Feast.
A BAND will play occasionally,

After the Concert, A BALL.

To begin precisely at SEVEN o'Clock.
Tickets may be had at Mr. GIBSON's.

(Gibson, Printer, Malton.)

This Vocal Concert was held on Thursday 30th
December 1813 and followed by a ball.

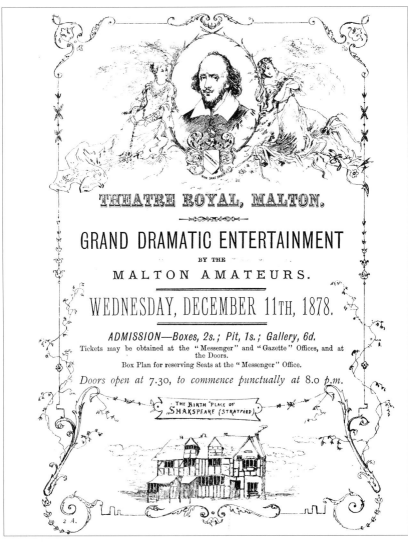

THEATRE ROYAL, MALTON,

GRAND DRAMATIC ENTERTAINMENT

BY THE

MALTON AMATEURS.

WEDNESDAY, DECEMBER 11TH, 1878.

ADMISSION—Boxes, 2s.; Pit, 1s.; Gallery, 6d.

Tickets may be obtained at the "Messenger" and "Gazette" Offices, and at the Doors.

Box Plan for reserving Seats at the "Messenger" Office.

Doors open at 7.30, to commence punctually at 8.0 p.m.

THE BIRTH PLACE OF SHAKSPEARE (STRATFORD)

Theatre Royal Malton programme, for shows, Dead Witness and Area Belle, held on Wednesday December 11th 1878.

Trinity Male Voice Choir, c. 1940s.

The Devec Singers, Norton, c. 1956. 'Devec' was an abbreviation of the first letters of the participating members. They are, left to right: Doreen Dobson, Eveline Danby, Vera Plumber, Ernest Biggs, Charles Johnson. The man standing on the far right is John Marwood.

The Jovial Concert party, c. 1938.

Carrie Baker's Band in the Empire Ballroom (Dewhirst Clothing Factory) c. 1927-8. They also played in the Coronation Rooms, Commercial Street. Left to right. Reg Strangeway, Ron Rollinson, Mrs Baker (pianist), Sam Tong, Frank Robinson, Alec Strangeway.

The 1956 pantomime, *The House That Jack Built*. Left to right: Mary Lythe, Ann Johnson, Eva Ashcroft, Joan Layton, Dudley Wallis, Ena Smith, Pearl Stone, Peter Paylor, Rita Bowes.

The 1955 pantomime, *Babes in the Wood*. Alwyna Hale was Robin Hood and Doreen Willis was Maid Marion.

The 1952 pantomime, *Cinderella*. Left to right: W. Little, (producer and writer of many Malton pantos) Joan Layton, Dudley Wallis and Marjorie Cartwright.

Ena Smith and Horace Cryer as Pearly King and Queen, were founder members of the Malton and Norton Amateur Operatic Society.

St Peter's Players, *But Once a Year*, 1948. Left to right: Harry Burrows, Laura Stockdale, Beatrice Driver, Norman Jefferson, Jose Moore, Sturley Wood, Sylvia Star, Charles Cryer, Myra Hayton, Beatrice Rowsby.

St Peter's Players, *The Chiltern Hundreds*, 1951. Left to right: Charles Berry, Ruth Thorpe, John Grey, Patrica Frankish, William Frankish, Laura Stockdale, Sturley Wood, Jean Gray.

Trinity Bright Hour, c. 1944-46. The first meeting was held in Bethel schoolroom. The meeting then had in the region of 120 members.

Malton Girl Guides on parade for the Coronation in 1953.

The York Musical Competitions were held on Friday-Saturday, 12th–13th May 1905, when Malton Male Voice Choir took first prize in their class, beating Michael-le-Belfry Choir of York.

Royal Antediluvian Order of Buffaloes Lodge. This picture was taken before 1929.

The 6th East Riding Battalion of the Home Guard at the Company Headquarters in Norton in September 1944.

Seven

Sport

Malton United 1925–26 beat Norton St Peter's 3 - 0 on Malton showground and were known as the Black and White Zebras. Back row, left to right: Freddie Lythe, Abby Taylor, Tom Cuthbertson, Tom Bell, Bill McGee, Jack Wood, Basil (Otto) Hudson. Middle row, left to right: Alf Wray, Calam Williamson, Cyril (Gash) Waller, Squire Hogg, Cyril Paylor. Front row, left to right: Victor Dallamore, Steve Woodall, Mac McBlain, Harry Buckle, Herbert Hodgson.

Malton Bible Club team, 1912–13.

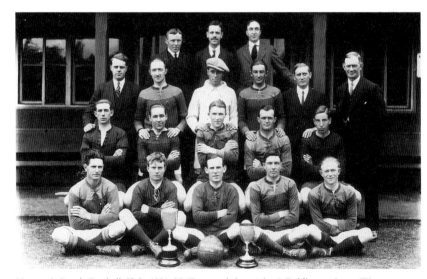

Norton St Peter's Football Club, 1921–22. Top row, left to right: J. Fieldhouse, Lance Watson, Mr Cascoign. Top Centre: Mr Preston, E. Leatham, E. Brocklass, Mr Milson, Mr Wilson, Mr Kitching. Bottom Centre: Mr Nendick, Mr Wompra, Mr Lumley, Mr Atkinson, Mr McCowan. Front row: G. Baker, M. Brown, Mr Cartwright, S. Witty, O. Smith.

Old Malton Cricket Club, still going strong in 1995.

Curling. This picture was taken at the Curling Rink, behind Malton Cricket Club.

Malton curlers brought world-wide fame in 1907, when they won for Britain the International Curling Bonspiel at the Swiss Winter Sports at Kanderstegg. This picture is of the Malton team outside the Royal Oak Public House with left to right: Mr John Potter (landlord of the Royal Oak), Mr William I'Anson (racehorse trainer), and Mr William Wilkinson (aerated water manufacturer).

The Talbot Bowling Club,° 1897. Back row: J. W. Atkinson, A. Brown, W. I'Anson, E. Eardsley, J. B. Harper, M. Williamson, W. Robinson, M. Pigg. Middle row: S. Kirk, G. Read, G. Aitken, R. Boulton, W. Roberts, T. Leefe, W. Cooper, S. Wallgate. Front row: J.H. Saxby, E.W. Tinsley, T. Bruckshaw, J. Read, E.K. Spielgelhalter, T. Longster, J. Fagan, F. Rand.

Malton Town Hockey Club 1913/4, a club which still runs successful mens' and womens' teams.

Eight

Schooldays

Malton Infants was built in 1837.

Norton Grove Street, Top Class Infants. The headmistress was Miss Mason and teacher, Miss Walker.

Malton Wesleyan day school. Class St VII, 1909.

Malton Wesleyan, St IV, 1922.

St Michael's School, a private girls' school. The principal was Miss Hobson. Girl's under twelve years paid twelve guineas per term; girls over twelve years fourteen guineas per term. The school is now The Mount Hotel.

Norton Bower Memorial Parochial School in Commercial Street was built 1873 and enlarged in 1899. The library now occupies this site.

The Wesleyan School was built in 1837 in Greengate and it has now been partly demolished.

Old Malton School has now been converted into houses.

Education.

W. COATES

Has taken and entered upon the School-Room in *Greengate*, lately occupied by R. Bull, and will commence Teaching in the same on Monday next.

W. C. is acquainted with the just principles of *Penmanship*; *Arithmetic*, and *practical Mathematics*; and flatters himself that he is in some degree qualified to initiate Youth in the *English Grammar*; he has, besides, had an opportunity of being instructed in an approved method of Teaching; and therefore hopes he shall meet with encouragement, not only from the Public in general, but also from the Friends of his Predecessor.

TERMS—PER QUARTER.

	s.	d.		s.	d.
READING	4	0	ARITHMETIC	6	0
WRITING	5	0	MATHEMATICS	8	0

Entrance, One Shilling.

Malton, Oct. 16, 1806.

J. GIBSON, PRINTER, MALTON.

An advertisement for a new school opened by Mr W. Coates in 1806.

Nine

Country Houses

Castle Howard. The 3rd Earl of Carlisle commissioned Sir John Vanbrugh to design a great house in 1699. Vanbrugh was assisted by Hawksmoore and the house has stayed in the Howard family to the present day. It was partly damaged by fire in 1940.

Easthorpe Hall. James Hebden moved into the old house in 1755 and rebuilt it. His grandson sold it to the Castle Howard Estate. Charles Smithson lived here in the 1840s and his friend Charles Dickens visited. Lord Grimthorpe had the hall in the 1920s and moved out in 1965. It latterly became a nightclub and was burnt down in 1971.

HILDENLEY MALTON 2

Hildenley. William Strickland acquired the estate in 1565 and it passed down to his descendant, Sir Charles Strickland Bt who died in 1909. It was then bought by the Hon. Francis Dawnay and was largely demolished soon after.

Slingsby Castle. The Mowbrays had a castle here which was partly rebuilt in 1603 by
Sir Charles Cavendish, it passed through many hands and fell into decay. The ruins were later
bought by the Castle Howard Estate.

HUTTONS-AMBO HALL
PHOTO BY JORDISON FILEY

Huttons Ambo Hall. Home of the late Col. Starkey.

Burythorpe House was owned by William Preston in 1840.

The Hall, Kirkham Abbey. In 1856, Kirkham belonged to Edward Clough Taylor Esq., whose seat is a handsome mansion built in 1839.

Howsham Hall was built in 1610 by William Bamburgh. Nathaniel Cholmley inherited both the Howsham and Whitby Estates in 1755. Howsham Hall is now a preparatory school.

Wold Cottage has been one of the principal racing establishments, having many owners from the 1840s: John Shepherd then, James Perren, James Fagan, William Sanderson, William Binnie, Walter Pollock, and others.